Shut Up, You're Fine!

Shut Up, You're Fine!

POEMS FOR VERY, VERY BAD CHILDREN

by Andrew Hudgins

Drawings by Barry Moser

The Overlook Press
New York

First published in the United States in 2009 by
The Overlook Press, Peter Mayer Publishers, Inc.
New York

NEW YORK:
141 Wooster Street
New York, NY 10012

Copyright © 2009 by Andew Hudgins
Illustrations © 2009 by Barry Moser

Cataloging-in-Publication Data is available from the Library of Congress

Book design by Barry Moser
Manufactured in the United States of America
ISBN 978-1-59020-103-9
FIRST EDITION
10 9 8 7 6 5 4 3 2 1

ACKNOWLEDGMENTS

AMERICAN POETRY REVIEW: "Our Neighbors' Little Yappy Dog," "Satan."

ANTIOCH REVIEW: "Clouds," "Cousin Marbury's Marvelous Bombs," "His Imaginary Friend," "Pacifist."

Boulevard: "Great Granny," "Goodbye to All This," "The Joys of Christmas Day," "The Starving Kids in Africa."

CRAZYHORSE: "Kiss Grandma Goodnight," "Magic," "The Night Wind," "One, Two."

THE DARK HORSE: The Scottish-American Poetry Journal: "Dead Things I Have Seen," "Grandmama's Teeth," "My Sister's Stash," "Why I Love Ruby."

GREAT RIVER REVIEW: "Had It Coming."

GREEN MOUNTAINS REVIEW: "Prayer."

THE HOPKINS REVIEW: "I Rode My Bike Over Hill and Dale," "Margaret and Her Puppy Ralph," "Spit Shine."

THE INDIANA REVIEW: "Daddy, Are We Meat?"

THE IOWA REVIEW: "My Mother Predicts Travel to Exotic Destinations."

THE NEW REPUBLIC: "The Boy in the Wheelchair."

MARGIE: "I'd Hate To Be An Astronaut."

THE OXFORD AMERICAN: "My Deepest Heart's Desire."

THE PARIS REVIEW: "When Granddad Says Please Kill Me," "We Buried the Cat but the Dog Dug Her Up."

POETRY: "At Camp," "Jim the Car," "The Cow," "The Glass Hammer," "Playing Dead," "Prayer Before Bed."

RIVER STYX: "My Last Dream," "The Old Dog," "The Schlitz Malt Liquor Bull," "Surprise!"

SALMAGUNDI: "The Moon," "My Bed is Not a Boat," "Playing Houth."

SHENANDOAH: "The Circus in the Trees," "The Tooth Fairy."

SLATE: "As Seen on Television," "Desert Island."

THIRD COAST: "I Think of Being in the Grave," "The Thumping of the Bed."

TRIQUARTERLY: "Fat Johnny," "Grandmother's Bed," "My Hero," "The County Fair," "The Ice Cream Truck."

CONTENTS

1.

2.

3.

1.

There was a young poet of Thusis
Who took twilight walks with the Muses.
But these nymphs of the air
Are not quite what they were,
And the practice has led to abuses.

Anon. From W. H. Auden's
BOOK OF LIGHT VERSE.

I looked into the abyss and the abyss looked into me—
and neither of us liked what we saw.

Brother Theodore.

HAD IT COMING

Hush now—don't cry, my wayward son.
You couldn't see you were becoming
someone who'd study "Manual Arts"—
rough carpentry, not even plumbing.

Mother smelled, and Father too,
the cigarettes that you've been bumming.
We searched beneath your bed and found
the dirty books that you've been thumbing.

And what about your so-called friends,
the criminals and thugs you're chumming
around with at the Mini-mart?
They hang with you and think they're slumming.

And as we yelled, you shrugged and snorted,
eyeballs rolling, fingers drumming.
You sighed, picked up your guitar,
tuned, retuned it, started strumming.

Your father cursed, and slammed the door.
I slapped you till your head was humming.
Hush now—don't cry, my wayward son.
You little shit—you had it coming.

Kiss Grandma Goodnight

The old ones smell funny.
They don't smell of gum,
pie or pink candy,
but gardenia and mum.

They smell of white flowers,
huge, dying flowers,
and sometimes gin,
which kills the long hours.

They insist that you kiss
their sunken gray lips
before they hand over—
licorice whips?

They'll sulk all alone
and guzzle cheap gin,
or talk to dead husbands
to feel loved again.

But pucker and kiss them.
Act like a chum.
Lie that you love them.
They're what you'll become.

THE STARVING KIDS IN AFRICA

The starving kids in Africa,
would love the processed meat,
canned beets, and cold asparagus
that you're too good to eat.

Each night you see them on TV,
their bellies big and bloated,
and if I'd offered it to them
I'm sure they would have voted

to gobble up those Harvard beets
that you say make you sick—
although they're rich with vitamins,
and hypoallergenic.

Your father slaved to buy that Spam
and I slaved when I fried it
and when I see you bury it
with Tater Tots to hide it,

I'd love to ship your ass to Chad
and let some foreign brat
hide you inside his Tater Tots,
then slip you to the cat.

One, Two

One, two—
Eat cold stew.
Three, four—
Don't ask for more.
Five, six—
Hit the bricks.
Seven, eight—
You'll have to wait.
Nine, ten—
I don't know when.

Ten, nine—
Don't whimper and whine.
Eight, seven—
You'll eat in heaven.
Six, five—
What! Still alive?
Four, three—
Stop pestering me.
Two, one—
Supper's done!

The Moon

I think that it's creepy—the way that it changes,
the way that it changes and sneaks off at dawn.
Sometimes it's lopsided. Sometimes it's round.
Sometimes it's glowing, and sometimes it's gone.

The moon makes me nervous. I don't understand it.
It's made of green cheese, Granddaddy said.
But sometimes it's blue, and sometimes it's white.
and sometimes it's orange, like processed cheese spread.

I might like the moon if it didn't change.
If the moon didn't change, I think I'd adore it,
the way I love my Mommy and Daddy,
and as I do them, I could simply ignore it.

That's the moon's problem. Nobody can trust it.
Sometimes it's round and sometimes lopsided,
and sometimes it sprouts sharp points at each end.
It could put out your eye, and leave you glass-eyeded.

Uncle Jim, when he's drinking, tells me the full
moon is a white ass hung in the blue.
The new moon's a black ass and the quarter's the half
of his ass blown to heaven outside of Pleiku.

The moon must decide what it wants to be,
no matter how dangerous, butt-like, or strange.
Let the moon be the moon it likes the best.
But make it choose once and then never change.

Magic

The cracks on the sidewalk hold powerful magic.
Step on one once and your mom's paraplegic.

No one had told me. I walked without thought
on whether my sneakers touched cracks or not.

My dear mom writhing with a shattered back!
Her skin drooping slackly, her toes turning black!

But once I had heard of the cracks' awful power,
I placed my feet gingerly. Each step made me cower.

One morning, not watching, I tripped on a crack.
My god, I had broken my own mother's back!

I'd save her from suffering. I'd make the pain cease.
I'd caused it. I'd stop it. I could grant her release.

Between there and home, I stomped all the lines,
exploding them all like long-distance mines.

I ran in the house and searched for remains.
Mom was under the sink, cleaning the drains.

I was all set to cry, my face was tragic.
But Mom was alive. My world wasn't magic.

THE TOOTH FAIRY

Each time another tooth falls out,
I yearn to learn the truth
about what kind of crazy thief
swaps cash for my old tooth.

I'd like to catch her by surprise
when she flies near my bed.
If I could hold her in my hands,
I'd squeeze her tiny head
between my finger and my thumb
and ask her just one time
why Jason Farber gets a buck.
I only get a dime.

Hide-and-Seek with Mommy and Dad

When I play hide-and-seek with them,
I never make a peep,
and in the dark behind the couch
I often fall asleep.

"We'll never find that clever boy,"
Mom calls, and Dad agrees.
And then for hours they search their room.
Mom giggles. Dad says, "Please."

I hear her shout "Not now! Not there!
Oh, try this place instead!"—
then judging by the mattress squeaks,
they really check the bed.

I wonder why they like the game
although they never win.
"You're too smart for us," Dad says,
and Mommy kicks his shin.

Maybe next time I'll take a peek
at Daddy and my mommy
playing a game Dad jokes about
in which he hides salami.

DADDY, ARE WE MEAT?

"Daddy, are we meat?" Jane asked.
"Mommy, are we meat?"
Daddy hemmed and Mommy hawed
and both stared at their feet.

"Pretend I am a market pig.
Pretend I am a steer.
I know my shoulder is a brisket
and the rump roast is my rear.

"But where's my porterhouse and rib-eye?
My tenderloin and flank!
I want to know all my good cuts,
including cross-cut shank."

"Daddy, are we meat?" Jane asked.
"Mommy, are we meat?"
Her mom looked slightly queasy,
her dad slid down his seat.

That day, against her will, Sweet Jane
turned vegetarian.
A child who knows we all are meat
soon learns we're carrion.

ROVER

Rover's such a clumsy dog!
We love to laugh at Rover.
He topples in the toilet bowl
and somersaults in clover.

He's crazy to play leapfrog now
and the neighbor's dog loves Rover—
but Rover's always getting stuck
before he's halfway over!

THE SCHLITZ MALT LIQUOR BULL

When Daddy kills a quart of Schlitz,
he holds his fingers up like horns.
He snorts and bellows, paws the rug.
"I'm coming after you," he warns.

I hit the screen door screaming, "Help,"
race caterwauling through the grass,
but Daddy runs me till I fall
and his sharp fingers gore my ass.

He jabs me till I'm blubbering,
and then he gives my head a whack.
"You're such a little sissy-boy!"
he sighs, and throws me on his back.

"Now hold on tight—you're riding, son,
the Schlitz Malt Liquor bull!" He bucks
up-down, left-right, to-fro—before
he doubles up and then upchucks.

I wrench his right ear, slap his ass,
and clinging like death to his shirt,
shout, "Ride'm, cowboy, ride'm hard,"
and spur my Brahma to the dirt.

Apostrophes to Lunch

To a Flawless Slice of Bread

O flawless slice, I like you best
because your sandwich mate
is slightly smushed around the crust.
Please settle my debate.

Do you desire the top or base
of my baloney sandwich?
Should I bestow pink meat on you?
Or should I make a switch,

and slap the blemished bread face down
to hold my fried baloney,
then set you on it, like a crown,
with phony ceremony?

To a Platter of Frankfurters

"Which one of you is my favorite frank?"
I ask my sausage links.
"Which one of you should I eat first?"
I wonder what meat thinks.

What would I want if I were pork?
Is it a hot-dog honor
to be picked first or saved for last?
Whatever. You're a goner.

The Old Dog

Old Fred sleeps in the bed here beside me.
He farts, he stinks, and I think he's got worms:
ringworm and roundworm, hookworm and heartworm—
You can see them at night when his butt kinda squirms.

After a rain, when they crawl on the sidewalk,
he slurps up the earthworms. He must have those too.
I know he has fleas and he pees on himself,
and both his blind eyes ooze gobbets of goo.

Mama says he's so nasty we'll soon put him down.
I sniff at my armpits, and the stench makes me blink.
I've got fleas, maybe worms, and I pee in my sleep.
Each morning I wring out stained sheets in the sink.

I scrub them real quiet and remake the bed.
If Mama suspects me, I'm blaming Fred,
so Mama won't have me put down instead.
I'm sorry, old boy, but I'm planning ahead.

The Glass Hammer

My mother's knickknack crystal hammer
gleamed by her silver tray.
Oh pick me up and play with me,
I heard the hammer say.

I tapped it on the silver tray.
I tapped my sister's kitty.
"Put that thing down," my mother yelled.
"It's not a damn play-pretty."

Oh, I'm a hammer. Work with me,
the wicked hammer goaded.
I found a nail. I hit the nail.
The hammer, it exploded.

The doctors stitched my hands and face
and sewed up my right knee.
My mother gave me good advice.
The hammer lied to me!

The hammer said it was a tool,
although it couldn't hammer.
The better hammer was my mom,
who hammered me—goddamn'er.

PLAYING DEAD

Our father liked to play a game.
He played that he was dead.
He took his thick black glasses off
and stretched out on the bed.

He wouldn't twitch and didn't snore
or move in any way.
He didn't even seem to breathe!
We asked, Are you okay?

We tickled fingers up and down
his huge, pink, stinky feet—
He didn't move; he lay as still
as last year's parakeet.

We pushed our fingers up his nose,
and wiggled them inside—
Next, we peeled his eyelids back.
Are you okay? we cried.

I really thought he might be dead
and not just playing possum,
because his eyeballs didn't twitch
when I slid my tongue across 'em.

He's dead, we sobbed—but to be sure,
I jabbed him in the jewels.
He rose, like Jesus, from the dead,
though I don't think Jesus drools.

His right hand lashed both right and left.
His left hand clutched his scrotum.
And the words he yelled—I know damn well
I'm way too young to quote 'em.

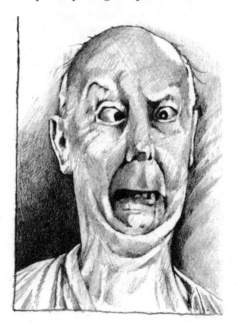

THE COW

I love the red cow
with all of my heart.
She's gentle when pulling
my cherry-red cart.

We take her rich milk
and swallow it down.
With nothing, it's white,
with chocolate, brown.

When she grows too feeble
to give us fresh cream,
we'll slit her red throat,
hang her from a beam,

and pull out her insides
to throw to the dogs,
just as we do
when we slaughter the hogs.

We've now owned six cows
that I can remember.
We drain them and gut them,
skin and dismember,

package and label them,
and stock up the freezer.
We all love beefsteak—
from baby to geezer!

Tossed on the grill,
the bloody steaks sputter.
As a last, grateful tribute,
so humble we stutter,

we offer up thanks
with a reverent mutter—
then slather her chops
with her own creamy butter.

My Bed is Not a Boat

My bed is a ship on a carpet of blue
as blue as the yearning sea.
I pitch all night on churning waves
I feel but cannot see.

When I awake at morning light
from sailing on the deep,
I find my boat has sprung a leak
and drenched me in my sleep.

Your bed is not a goddamn boat!
Mom yells—and I agree.
My body, it must be the boat
and my blue sheets the sea.

When I sail into port at dawn
with ballast tanks to drain,
I blow my bilge into the bay
in a spreading golden stain.

Mom yells my bed is just a bed,
exactly as it seems.
I think that's what she means to say.
Mostly she just screams.

I Rode my Bike
Over Hill and Dale

I rode my bike over hill and dale
and over rock and rill—
though I'm not sure I'd know a "dale"
as I zoomed down the hill

unless it had a sign on it
in big and bright-red print.
I might have recognized a rill
if given half a hint,

and I might be surprised to know
a fen, a lea, a mead
was something I saw every day
(and not just when I read)—

as I went flying down the hill
too fast to ask, "What's that?"
of all the things I hurtled past—
until I hit a cat.

I wobbled, fell, and broke my crown.
I learned it as it healed,
so now I know the blood-soaked skull
the schoolbook name concealed.

MY LAST DREAM

The last time I remember dreaming
I woke up in the black night screaming
about the wild dogs in the park.
They chased me through the moonless dark
and I could feel their cold, wet noses
sniffing at the printed roses
on my gown flapping down the street.
Forty wild dogs nipped my feet.
Shrieking out my desperate prayers,
I raced to my house, up the stairs,
and leapt into my narrow bed.
Forty wild dogs, their teeth red
from other children they had killed,
burst through the bedroom door and spilled
onto the bedspread over me.
Three were gnawing on my knee
when I woke in the black night screaming.
Mom and Daddy, their eyes gleaming
in the moonlight from the window,
said, "You've put on quite a show.
Don't let us hear another peep.
Shut the hell up and let us sleep."

The Night Wind

Wild Mister Wind drives a black eighteen-wheeler,
miles of dark metal and a thundering diesel.
He sprays you with rain while you're thumbing a ride
He blasts his huge air horn and spits greasy drizzle.

He stops, and you leap in the cab up beside him.
You laugh at your friends as you roar past their houses—
as you roar past their houses and blast the huge air horn
and startle their moms and stare down their blouses.

Mister Wind, Mister Wind, Wild Mister Wind,
he's all over the road and off the road too.
Maybe he's drinking or popping pep pills.
Maybe he's huffing airplane glue.

But Wild Mister Wind will buy you pink candy.
He'll pull down an alley where no streetlights burn.
He'll first touch you gently, then touch you harder.
He'll touch you all over and you'll never return.

THE THUMPING OF THE BED

The thump, thump, thump of the hideous bed
wakes me up late at night,
and for an hour it hammers at my wall
as I cower and cringe in fright.

The thump, thump, thump of the hideous bed
in Mommy and Daddy's room
tilts pictures on the picture hooks.
Often they fall with a boom.

Refrain:
Their headboard smacks the bedroom wall—
bang-a-bang, a-bang, bang, bang.
They maul each other in a walloping brawl—
a-bang, a-bang bang, a-bang bang.

The thump, thump, thump of the hideous bed
gives way to animal calls—
they grunt, they bark, they whinny and squawk.
A pig squeal rises and falls.

The thump, thump, thump of the hideous bed
peters out with a bleat like a sheep.
Then the demon possessing their souls
rolls over and we all fall asleep.

43

Refrain:

Their headboard smacks the bedroom wall--
bang-a-bang, a-bang, bang, bang.
They mall each other in a walloping brawl—
a-bang, a-bang bang, a-bang bang.

Plus, on the final refrain:

Bang-a-bang, a-bang, a-bang bang.

WITCH

We drove into the country,
way down a red-dirt track
then stumbled up a path,
and bushwhacked to a shack.

She only had one arm,
she only had one leg,
she only had one eye,
a bright-red Easter egg.

"Come here and hug your granny,"
the old witch squawked at me.
Go on! my mother whispered
and shoved me with her knee.

45

Did she have an understanding
to give me to the witch?
I'd heard of Rumplestiltskin.
My face began to twitch.

"Come to your loving granny,"
the old witch shrilly said.
Again my mother shoved me,
and this time smacked my head.

I inched away from Mom and Dad.
I swore I'd always hate 'em.
The witch smelled of used grease,
mildew and Mentholatum.

I struggled hard. I fought her.
I couldn't break her grip.
Who'd think it'd be so easy
to make a wheelchair tip?

The Dying Boy's Lament

Bury me deep with my jacks and my yo-yo,
bury me deep with my barely chewed gum
stuck to the side of my tiny black coffin.
That would be, like, totally awesome.

I'll miss my sweet gum but now I must leave it.
I'll miss the rich taste of grape-flavored gum.
I'll miss chocolate ice cream. I'll miss steaming cocoa.
And I'll never unwrap my top-secret condom.

Crack open the blacktop out on the playground.
Under the Jungle Gym, crack open macadam--
under the Jungle Gym: it was my favorite
until I jumped off and fractured my cranium.

Crack open the asphalt and slide in my coffin.
Then back up the truck and seal the macadam,
while old friends and new friends gather around
to snicker and mimic my terminal spasm.

No more will I swing from the hot Jungle Gym
—faster and faster, lit with delirium—
or run down the slide or dance on the seesaw.
O, Mother, I should have taken my lithium.

Death has chosen: "Send Tommy over!"
Death has called me and I have to come
racing across into Death's freezing arms.
Now, I'll shot hoops in Hades' gymnasium.

I'll play Red Rover on the playgrounds of Hades,
B-ball and kickball among the deep shades.

PRAYER BEFORE BED

Of course I pray for Mommy's health.
She fixes every meal.
I bless my sister—Mom insists—
though sometimes I conceal

an off-the-record prayer inside
the prayer my parents hear:
That Sister get a chronic rash—
well, chronic and severe.

But most of all I pray that God
keep Daddy safe and well,
that all the charges be dismissed
and that his used cars sell.

Make Daddy confident and glib
and keep his handshake firm
so when it's time to close the deal
the suckers never squirm.

Lord, keep his commissions high
so I won't have to kneel
with nose to grindstone, ear to ground,
and shoulder to the wheel.

I couldn't work in that stance, Lord,
or polish pitted chrome.
As much as I love bacon, Lord,
let Daddy bring it home.

2.

THE CIRCUS IN THE TREES

I love to watch the gray squirrels leap
from limb to leafy limb,
tumbling like furry acrobats—
and every tree their gym.

The oak limbs are their trampoline,
and their trapeze the pines.
They stroll, like tightrope walkers, up
the looping power lines—

and sometimes they gnaw through a line,
exploding as it arcs,
and lighting up the evening sky,
cascading down as sparks.

SWASHBUCKLER

I'd like to be a buccaneer.
I'd wear a black eye patch
and I could really use a hook
as often as I scratch.

I'd call my talking parrot Sam.
That's my brother's name.
And I'd make Sam sing jaunty songs
of my swashbuckling fame.

I'd strut my deck with a peg-leg thump
while my brother walked the plank,
then I'd watch him splash and beg,
and toast him as he sank!

WHY I LOVE RUBY

When Mom dated lawyers,
they showed me their briefs,
and the preacher she dated
held secret beliefs:

We knelt by the bed
and asked the Almighty
to forgive us our sins
and send Mom a silk nightie.

Now Mom's dating Ruby—
What wonderful luck!
We roar around town
in her half-ton truck.

We wash it together,
polish the chrome,
and she doesn't touch me
when she drives me home.

When a biker downtown
called me a fairy,
her face turned as red
as Mom's Bloody Mary.

She rolled up the sleeves
of her plaid cutoff shirt,
kneed the guy's balls,
rubbed his face in the dirt.

Not till he looked up,
did I see it was Dad!
He called her a dyke,
and made it sound bad.

Though the preacher once told me
her sins defile her,
I love her spiked boots
and adore her Rottweiler.

Dead Things I Have Seen

I've seen a thousand possum skins
pancaked on the road,
a hundred armadillo humps,
and flat squirrels by the load.

But I don't think it's fair to count
meat once it's in the kitchen,
though if it's in the slaughterhouse
you can count pork or chicken.

I don't count Daddy's big-mouth bass
that's hanging on the wall
or Uncle Bill's stuffed threadbare moose
bought at the antique mall.

The deer Mom clobbered with the car—
that counts, and counts big time,
because I saw its tongue stick out,
and its nose drip yellow slime.

I count my sister's parakeet, which chirped
a frightened chirp and died,
increasing scientific knowledge
the afternoon I tried

to see how far his head would turn
before he crossed the bar.
Three hundred and fifty-two degrees
is one degree too far.

But I don't count Aunt Mary Jean,
since lying cold and coffined,
she looked less mean and more alive
and her frown had slightly softened.

SPIT SHINE

My mama grabbed my chin and stared.
She licked her rough right thumb.
She moved it hugely toward my face
and homed in on a crumb.

I cringed and tried to hide my face.
She yanked me to my toes,
and her spit-icky thumb flicked off
some dried Spaghetti-Os.

She rubbed me red, scrubbed me raw
and buffed me till I bled,
before she stepped back half a step,
admired her work, and said,

"You look a little better now!"
Well, thank you, Dr. Jekyll.
"That scrape'll heal, and anyhow
I never liked that freckle."

I Think of Being in the Grave

I think of being in the grave.
        I think of my tight coffin.
I think of living underground
        and feeling my skin soften.

My guts will swell until they pop,
        my black eyeholes will stare.
The white bones hidden by my skin
        will dry and crack in air.

When I am done imagining,
        I pray a long, long prayer
so God will know I'm happy here
        at least compared to there.

Margaret and Her Puppy Ralph

Margaret dressed her puppy Ralph
in Mom's hot-pink beret.
She draped pink ribbons on his neck
and knelt with him to pray.

He wiggled in her chubby arms
and tried to lick her face
when she dressed him in flannel gowns
adorned with bright pink lace.

But as her puppy Ralph grew up,
he chewed her flannel gown.
He gnawed off Barbie's legs and head—
then knocked poor Margaret down.

He licked her salty tears away
while she curled on the ground,
wept, hiccuped, sobbed, and caterwauled.
So Mom drove to the pound.

And Margaret stared across the seat
and studied like a scholar
the chewed and faded shred of pink
still hanging from Ralph's collar

When I Grow Up

Daddy brings home legal pads,
but Mommy brings home gauze,
used needles, and heart monitors,
like toys from Santa Claus.

Aunt Netty brings us pens from work.
Aunt Ruth on Christmas day
provides our turkey and our tree.
Thank you, IGA!

When his night foreman's out of town,
my uncle Bobby Lee
drives Daddy's van to Tune and Lube
and swaps out tires for free.

Some cousin on Sears' loading dock
shipped us a vinyl floor,
but I can't wait to land a job
at Kleinman's jewelry store:

I've got my eye on wedding bands
so Dad can marry Mom
or at least not take another date
to Mom's third junior prom.

CLOUDS

I love to lie out in the yard
and watch the clouds float by.
That one's like a wrestling ring—
and there's a butterfly.

And that one's like the coach's truck
when he stops by at three.
He greets Mom with a hug and kiss.
The Kit Kat bar's for me.

That cloud's soft and billowy
just like the coach's rear
when he pins Mom in a shoulder lock.
And there's one like a deer!

PACIFIST

I said I was a pacifist.
I wouldn't kill a flea.
All living things are sanctified—
at least as much as me.

But ants kept running underneath
my shoes, to my regret.
Mom gave me pinworm medicine,
and gnats drowned in my sweat.

Mosquitoes landed on my neck.
I slapped before I thought.
And when I saw my bloody palm
I wasn't overwrought.

My baseball glove is made of skin
stripped from a cow, and dried—
The chicken in my chicken pie
is not a suicide.

I'll stuff my mouth with misery
splendidly prepared,
and pray no fly is looking on
and that no mouse is scared.

I'll chew the suffering to paste,
deploring my delight,
then be a pacifist again
until tomorrow night.

THE ICE-CREAM TRUCK

From blocks away the music floats
to my enchanted ears.
It builds. It's here! And then it fades—
and I explode in tears.

I kick the TV set, and scream,
sobbing to extort her,
while Mom stares at *One Life to Live,*
and won't give me a quarter.

I pause, change tactics, snatch a coin
from the bottom of her purse,
then race to catch the ice-cream truck,
ignoring Mama's curse.

I stop the truck, I start to choose—
then see I won't be eating.
I stare down at a goddamn dime,
and trudge home to my beating.

As Seen on Television

If Daddy held a steady job
I'd learn my long division.
I'd be a smiling Kool-Aid kid—
as seen on television.

If Mom cooked supper every night,
I'd know Dred Scott's decision,
like a four-eyed geek on College Bowl—
as seen on televison.

If Daddy didn't drink all night,
I'd be a boy physician,
just like that Doogie Howser kid—
as seen on television.

If Mommy didn't cry all day,
I'd speak like a Parisian,
or at least as well as the ardent skunk—
as seen on television.

Surprise!

I slouched behind the kitchen door.
I lay behind the couch,
beneath the car, beside the hedge—
then I sprang from my crouch.

I bellowed like a gut-shot bull
when someone old walked by
because I loved to see Mom jump
and make that little cry

that sounds just like the parakeet
when someone plucks its tail.
My granddad reeled and grabbed his chest,
and Daddy, who'd jumped bail,

leapt out the nearest window, ran,
and we haven't seen him since,
except for one long strip of skin
left on the chain-link fence.

When I raced screaming through her room,
Grandma spat out her bridge.
The dentures flew across the room,
slick with mucilage.

Before they even hit the rug,
she grabbed me by both ears
and gummed my nose until I pledged
a mum, dumb, glum ten years.

Playing Houth

I loved playing houth with Rebecca Kothwinkle
Thee firth let me kith her, then puthed me away.
I begged. She thaid no. And then thee thaid maybe.
I rubbed up againth her and tharted to thway.

I pulled up her thkirt and thee puthed it down.
Up-down, up-down, up-down went the thkirt,
then down plunged her pantieth and up flew her bra,
and off went my thues, my thocks, and my thirt.

I never thought my thweetie'd agree!
My penith thriveled to the thize of a thnail.
"Oh, Becky, pleathe, pleathe thuck my penith!"
She laughed so hard she couldn't ekthale.

The more I thaid it, the harder thee thnickered.
"My penith won't thquirt you. Oh, Becky, I promith!"
But Rebecca Kothwinkle was done playing houth
and left me contholing a thullen John Thomath.

I'd Hate to Be an Astronaut

I'd hate to be an astronaut,
although it would be cool
to sleep while floating upside down
and not get up for school.

I'd fly above dumb foreign boys
that I am cooler than.
I'd stare down through the thin white clouds,
spit on Jerkoffistan,

and all the oddball countries I
misspelled on last week's quiz,
and let those Jerkistanis dread
when I'd take my next whiz.

Though I could dress in puffy clothes
and float around the moon
like some old-fashioned cartoon dog
turned Macy's Day balloon,

I'd hate to be an astronaut
because there's no debating,
a boy needs time alone when he's,
you know, uh....

The Blue-Tailed Skink's Blue Tail

In noonday sun, the skink's blue tail,
glittered blue on the white porch rail.

A skink would make a real swell pet—
at least for a minute or two, I'd bet.

I reached and grabbed, juggled and lost him,
grabbed again, and then sort of tossed him

into oak leaves slithering quicker
than I could pinch his electric flicker.

He left behind his dazzling tail
a blue and twitching, hectic flail.

In a more and more arthritic rhythm
between my finger and my thumb,

the blue drained from it bit by bit.
The gray whip slowed and almost quit.

I stuck the tail beneath my nose,
tickled by its dying throes,

till it produced a final thrash,
as I was twirling a dead moustache.

My Hero

My uncle takes me fishing
and to the picture show,

and when he looks at me
I see his tanned face glow.

Next weekend is the circus,
and I can't wait to go.

He promised me an ice cream—
and an extra Oreo

if I fumble in his pocket
and pull it out real slow.

He asks about my girlfriends
and calls me Romeo—

then winks a naughty wink,
whistles sly and low,

and chuckles when I blush.
He's only kidding though.

I've heard him in the hallway,
walking tippy-toe

and listening at my door.
He thinks that I don't know

he's checking up on me.
He's anguished at my woe

since he gave me a book
by Edgar Allen Poe.

Why else would he stand there,
trembling in his Speedo?

He says I'll have to wait
another year or so,

so I won't still be sobbing
at bricked-up Fortunato

and Berenice's teeth
scattered to and fro,

when I go and sleep over
with him and his friend Joe.

We'll all wear feather boas,
watch the video,

and I bet I won't be scared by
The Rocky Horror Show

because I love show tunes:
"Oklahoma," "Oh,

What a Beautiful Morning,"
and telling Dolly hello.

Dad shuffles through the kitchen
muttering, "No, no, no!"

when Joe and I belt "Mame"
in a giggling tremolo!

But Mommy laughs and joins us
for "It Ain't Necessarily So."

WE BURIED THE CAT
BUT THE DOG DUG HER UP

We buried the bird but the cat dug her up,
cat dug her up, cat dug her up,
we buried the bird but the cat dug her up—
so we got in the car and smashed her flat.
What do you think of that?

We buried the cat but the dog dug her up,
dog dug her up, dog dug her up.
We buried the cat but the dog dug her up—
so we got in the car and smashed her flat.
What do you think of that?

We buried the dog but the kids dug him up,
kids dug him up, kids dug him up,
we buried the dog but the kids dug him up—
so we got in the car and smashed him flat.
What do you think of that?

We buried the kids but the cops dug them up
cops dug them up, cops dug them up,
we buried the kids but the cops dug them up—
so we'll sit in the chair where Ted Bundy sat.
What do you think of that?

PRAYER

God who made the wind and rain,
who makes the blood pulse in my veins
and makes me vomit on jet planes—
please send my brother to Fort Wayne
so I can steal his girlfriend Jane.

God who makes my nose drip snot,
who made my pet cat die and rot
and made Jane such a ripe sexpot—
please help me master my hook shot.
so Jane will think I'm really hot.

Please drive Jane's family off a bend—
or come somehow to a bad end.
And while she's grieving, I intend
to help her shattered spirit mend.
She'll naturally become my girlfriend.

I ask this all on bended knee.
Or from my list of thirty-three,
please choose, dear Lord, another beauty
whose entire family's death would be
acceptable, dear God, to thee.

3.

Cousin Marbury's Marvelous Bombs

We stuff the tennis balls with caps,
  and pack lead pipes with cherry bombs.
We cram a coffee can with shotgun shells—
And when we set them off, amid the fumes
    we'll hear the booms
        as loud as Vietnam's.

My cousin said I mustn't tell
  the cops, our fathers or our moms
about the hand grenades or dynamite.
    And when we set them off, amid the fumes
    we'll hear the booms
        as loud as Vietnam's.

"I won't go back to jail," he swears.
    He laughs, and suddenly he calms
        and vows, "We'll kill them all. I got no qualms."
    And when we set them off, amid the fumes
    we'll hear the booms
        as loud as Vietnam's.

GRANDMAMA'S TEETH

Each night she takes herself apart
and puts what's left to bed.
Her hair goes on a little stand
shaped like a human head.

She wipes her arched eyebrows away,
peels off her jet-black lashes
and mounts them in their plastic case
like stockpiled flirty glances.

She scrubs her scarlet lipstick off
and her lips disappear
onto a piece of toilet paper
in a brilliant crimson smear

that circles in the toilet bowl
then slips down the abyss
with a loud slurping liquid sound
just like Grandmother's kiss.

With cold cream she returns her skin
to a grayer shade of death
and coats herself with Vapo-Rub
till I can't catch my breath.

Next she unplugs her hearing aid
and plucks the coarse gray wires
that sprout and bristle from her ears.
She uses Daddy's pliers.

She pops the lenses off her eyes
and packs them for the night
before she reaches toward her mouth.
I squeal with raw delight.

With a slow, teasing hand she grips
her upper two incisors,
pulls out her dentures, rinses them,
and applies her moisturizers.

I ooh and ah, coo and cluck,
listening to her troubles,
so she will let me sit up late
and watch the foaming bubbles

rise through her imitation teeth,
and artificial gums.
I study that pink plastic smile
till the half-grin becomes

the face her face will turn into
when she is in the grave.
The half-grin grins its haughty grin
and I pretend I'm brave.

The County Fair

I breezed by bumper cars
and past the Ferris wheel
and found the roller coaster
because I love to squeal

as the cars clank slowly upward,
groaning near the top,
before the screaming falters
and—one, two, three—we drop!

From gut to gullet, shudders
trembled through my chest
each time we cleared a peak
and clattered down the crest.

I stopped and ate a snow cone,
a deep-fried Chocolate Swirl,
a corn dog, half a pickle—
then rode the tilt-a-whirl.

I tilt-a-whirled three times
and roller-coastered four
before I found the sideshows
and started to explore.

I watched a man eat razors,
a lady sawn in half,
the crawfish boy, a dwarf or two,
and one six-legged calf.

I watched a woman strip
to a shiny black silk scrap
before I saw her beard
and upchucked on my lap.

The Joys of Christmas Day

On Christmas Day I am surprised
if I'm surprised—because
I've already opened every gift
from Grandmas and Grandpas.

I've rummaged Daddy's underwear
and under Mama's bras,
before I raked through Daddy's tools
and underneath his saws,

searching out the "useful" gifts
they'll blame on Santa Claus—
white shirts, white socks, loose underwear,
and two plaid mackinaws.

One fits, and one's to grow into.
Three cheers and two hurrahs.
For weeks before Saint Nick appears,
I'm blue. I've got the blahs.

I'm feeling worse and worse each day.
I know that guilt's the cause.
But guilt's just Jesus showing off.
You think he wants applause?

I stand before the mirror, smile,
and watch my smile for flaws,
rehearsing, "Thank you, thank you, yes!"
through clenched and aching jaws.

DESERT ISLAND

What would you take to a desert isle,
my teacher wanted to know.
I told her my Bible. That made her smile.
A copy of Robinson Crusoe!

She liked that one too. I mentioned my dog.
And pictures of Mamma and Pa.
She sniffled. Her glasses started to fog.
She sighed, and even said aaaah.

I mentioned my schoolbooks, and gave her a grin.
She looked at me and squinted.
She wanted the truth? Ten barrels of gin
and every *Penthouse* printed.

Our Neighbors' Little Yappy Dog

Our neighbors' little yappy dog
yaps all day on their lawn.
At dusk it takes a little nap
so it can yap till dawn.

At breakfast, sleepless, we make plans.
Mom says she wants to shoot it
while Dad wants to snatch the brute,
and, like a football, boot it.

And if it cleared the power line,
he'd raise his arms and call,
It's up, it's straight, it's good. Three points!
Of course he'd spike the ball.

But in the end we all agree
my plan will leave it deader.
I want to feed it—tail-first, slowly—
into the chipper-shredder.

His Imaginary Friend

I meet her twice a day for tea.
We talk about the weather,
her dolls, my love for her, her dolls,
and how we're good together.

We smile. I take her dainty hand
and beg a little kiss,
and then I peck her on the lips
and linger in the bliss.

I whisper to my fantasy,
"I want to more than kiss you"—
before I consummate my love
in Kleenex facial tissue.

THE BOY IN THE WHEELCHAIR

When I am walking down the hall
gossiping with friends,
Walter motors up behind
and wallops our rear ends.

Our books go flying in the air,
we crumple to the ground,
while Walter points at us and laughs
before he zips around

our bodies twitching on the floor,
taking special care
to crush our outstretched fingers
as he rolls past in his chair.

He's broken Betty Thompson's leg
and Harold Snyder's knees.
and sidelined half the football team
with ankle injuries.

Each night when I'm alone in bed
I pray to God and beg
that Walter will be healed and walk
so I can break his leg.

MY GRANDMOTHER'S BREASTS

My grandmother's breasts
were too big for her chest,
so they hung ninety years to her knees.
They wouldn't stay compressed
since they busted out her dress
every time the old girl had to sneeze.

As they swung side to side,
they could brush you aside—
she was mammaries personified.
But they swung last,
never to swing again,
when the old girl died.

Ninety years pendulumming:
ta-boom, ta-boom;
gazongas conga-drumming:
ta-boom, ta-boom;
But they swung last, never to swing again,
when the old girl died.

In watching gedoinkers
bobble up and down,
I spent many hours while a boy.
Out on the town,
I found it profound
to ogle them and slobber with joy.

My grandmother's tits
frightened me to bits,
though grown men gaped at them and sighed.
But they swung last,
never to swing again,
when the old girl died.

Ninety years pendulumming:
ta-boom, ta-boom;
gazongas conga-drumming:
ta-boom, ta-boom;
But they swung last, never to swing again,
when the old girl died.

FAT JOHNNY

Fat Johnny's mom re-nailed the pantry door.
re-locked the fridge, re-emptied the bread bin,
returned un-nibbled Snickers to the store.
Fat Johnny's on a diet once again.

She checked beneath his bed. The sight was chilling.
Where did the green-fur on the rug begin
to turn to blue fur on the donut filling?
Fat Johnny's on a diet once again.

Mom sighed, and said she'd buy more cottage cheese.
Alone, Fat Johnny slipped into the den.
His stomach fluttered like a hive of bees.
Fat Johnny's on a diet once again.

The sofa yielded Zotz, four TV clickers,
nine un-popped popcorn kernels, one pork skin,
and something that looked, but didn't taste, like Snickers.
Fat Johnny's on a diet once again.

Her home's so clean Mom canned the cleaning service.
But Johnny's starving. He has a ravenous yen.
And Minnie the guinea pig is looking nervous.
Fat Johnny's on a diet once again.

Mom loves how Johnny licks the cabinets clean:
and the floor's as shiny as it's ever been—
though she wonders why she's low on Vaseline.
Even Fat Johnny can't chew a dry saltine!
Fat Johnny's on a diet once again.

MY SISTER'S STASH

Trying on my sister's bra,
I found her stash. Hooray! Hurrah!
I stared at it and sang with awe,
Tra la—lalalala!

Tucked in the right cup of her bra—
a little gift from Bogota!
I laughed until I strained my jaw.
Tra la—lalalala!

The snitchy bitch who told Grandma
I'd glued tacks on the school seesaw,
now lives, like me, outside the law.
Tra la—lalalala!

I can stay home in Omaha
inside my private Shangri-la.
Goodbye, dear Omaha—aloha!
Tra la—lalalala!

GOODBYE TO ALL THIS

My mom and dad will soon come back,
and snatch me from these tacky people
who keep insisting they're my folks.
Mom and Dad, while I'm asleep'll

sweep me off and I'll awake
in Paris, Buenos Aires, Rome—
just any place but Terre Haute,
on an estate sans garden gnome!

Or so I'd hoped till Saturday.
As *Rock Star* then *The Real World* blared,
I slumped before the TV set,
and, sick with lost hope, I compared

my face to Mom's and Dad's, six aunts',
and thirteen cousins' catfish chins
receding under catfish eyes
and oblong, fat-lipped catfish grins.

I checked, re-checked and checked again,
and every time, I looked like them.
Beneath each nose there hung a mole
big as a orange M&M.

Goodbye to working just one job.
Goodbye to living as virgin.
I got to earn the kind of bread
that buys a topnotch plastic surgeon.

JIM THE CAR

He sputters his lips with a guttural rumble,
a V-8 blast, plus a timing-belt stumble.

He down-shifts to third and floors the gas,
slews sideways, corrects it, and pulls out to pass

two drag-assing fat girls blocking the hall
like side-by-side big rigs slowed to a crawl.

"They ought to print 'Wide Load' on their asses.
They're holding up traffic. I'm late for my classes."

He bleats like an air horn and flips them the bird
as they blink their eyes, not sure what's occurred.

He squeals—laying rubber! His racing slicks spin.
"That weirdo belongs in the state loony bin!"

The second girl says, "I guess it's car-thotic."
The first girl replies, "It's auto-erotic."

He zooms down the hallway, bends into curves,
and, revving his engine, he up-shifts and swerves

toward algebra class, not hearing their jeers.
Roaring louder and louder, he winds through the gears.

They're gone, they're behind him, they're history, they're lost.
He's a 4 4 0 hemi with a glass-pack exhaust.

My Mother Predicts Travel to Exotic Destinations

Shut up and study harder.
You'd have to be a fool
to get these grades. Another F
and it's military school.

Or better yet, enlist—
and let the army feed you.
Then you can gripe about their food
and what they guaranteed you.

All you do is snarl—
and stomp downstairs for chow
You're eating us into the poorhouse.
You're like a garbage scow.

Yes, all you do is eat—
and chase your cheap blonde slut.
Do you think that minx will visit you
when the prison door slams shut?

If you tried, you might enjoy
a girl who studies books,
holds down a steady job—or two—
and maybe even cooks—

even if she lacks dyed hair
and fake breasts like that tart
who'll have you stealing from the till
and robbing Quickee-Mart

to keep her pimp in cocaine
and her babies in day-care.
You know she'll be with someone else
when they strap you in the chair.

Only Mom will be there
when you lose your last appeal—
to tell you not to gulp your food
when you eat your final meal.

My Deepest Heart's Desire

When I was just a boy
my deepest heart's desire
was eating chocolate icing—
all I could acquire.

But mother only let me
scrape clean the batter bowl
and that was not enough
to glut my greedy soul.

I yearned to make a batch
of double chocolate fudge
and spoon it in my mouth
until I couldn't budge.

But now I'm twenty-one,
in bars and drinking beer,
I ask for Miller Lite
so my grown friends won't sneer.

It wouldn't wow the willowy chicks
or boost my self esteem
if I ordered up a can of Hines
Chocolate Buttercream.

At Camp

Everyone says the deep woods are soothing—
you won't hear leaf-blowers or car sirens throbbing.
You'll slide into sleep to the singing of crickets,
untroubled by mowers or Mom's drunken sobbing.

While I lie in my tent, wind tears at the canvas,
and I hear something savage creeping outside,
scuffling the dry leaves and sniffing my trail.
Mom could sleep better, she said, if I died.

What is it that howls out there in the darkness?
What is it saying? Why does it prowl?
It loves the full moon, fresh meat and hot blood—
howling for howling, the best kind of howl.

Late Sunday night when my roommate's bare foot
awakened the green snake I'd hid in his bed,
he screamed, and I howled back a maniac's howl,
the shriek of a demon freed from my head.

The demon is me and I'm starting to like him.
He answers the night with a shriek from my bowel,
a howl for the moon, fresh meat and hot blood—
howling for howling, the best kind of howl.

Grandmother's Bed

At Grandmother's grave, I stood at her feet
and somersaulted onto her face.
If I'd worn golf shoes—that'd be sweet!

I love thinking of her in that cold place--
no blankets or night light, and nothing to eat,
with dirt as her pillow and her pillowcase.

Mom sniffled and cried. She said it was sweet
how time, God's love and forgiveness erase
the pain we'd suffered. What pain? It's a treat

the old witch ain't here hawking snot in the fireplace,
and croaking love songs to her parakeet.
After she died, I sprayed it with Mace

and laughed as it choked its last half-tweet.
It's the only witness that saw me replace
her heart pills with blue pills I bought down the street.

Since her heart hiccupped its final beat,
the bed's all mine, though cold as concrete
and the stale scent of lavender clings to the sheet.

SATAN

Do you have Satan in your heart?
the preacher asked. I did.
The demon kicked inside my groin.
I was a wicked kid.

In my aisle seat I sweated fear.
I had no doubt—still don't—
that Satan owned my sinful heart.
I staggered to the font.

The preacher lowered me to Death
then yanked me, gasping, up,
red-faced and dripping. After that,
I went to early worship—

and there I sat behind a boy
whose ear did not attach
entirely to his head, but left
an oblong pink mismatch.

Through that pink gap of flesh and gristle,
much like a rifle sight,
I lined the shouting preacher up
and tracked him left and right.

Each time he stopped to take a breath,
halting his harangue,
I squeezed my trigger finger tight.
I softly whispered, "Bang!"

WHEN GRANDDAD SAYS, "PLEASE KILL ME!"

He can't control his bowels
and since the stroke he drools,
and sings those dirty army songs
about the family jewels.

He tells you of his sores
and tries to make you look.
He tells you all his friends are dead
and he resents their luck.

Refrain:

When Granddad says, "Please kill me!"
you mustn't help him die—
no matter how he begs and pleads
and tries to tell you why.

No matter he's incontinent
and when he pees he bleeds—
just look him in the bleary eye—
deny him what he needs!

You can lay a knife beside him
and tell him what it's for,
but you cannot hold it to his throat
and then complete the chore.

You can prop pills on his pillow
fetch water by the quart
but you cannot help him swallow them,
though he's on life support.

Refrain:

When Granddad says, "Please kill me!"
you mustn't help him die—
no matter how he begs and pleads
and tries to tell you why.

No matter he's incontinent
and when he pees he bleeds—
just look him in the bleary eye—
deny him what he needs!

You can hand Granddad the gun
when you're a little bigger.
You can even click the safety off,
but you mustn't pull the trigger.

But if you find a plastic bag
pulled down across his nose,
feel free to shut the bedroom door
and leave on tippy-toes.

Refrain, plus legato:

When Granddad says, "Please kill me!"
you mustn't help him die—
no matter how he begs and pleads
and tries to tell you why.

No matter he's incontinent
and when he pees he bleeds—
just look him in the bleary eye—
deny him what he needs!

Yes, when Granddad says, "Please kill me!"
you mustn't help him die—
no matter how he begs and pleads
and tries to tell you why.

SLEEP, SLEEP

Sleep, sleep,
hard and deep.
Night has murdered telltale day.

Sleep, sleep
and try to keep
dreaming as bullets ricochet.

Bleep! bleep!
the trash trucks beep,
slamming down the alleyway.

Cheep, cheep,
house wrens peep
among syringes at break of day.

"Cheap! Cheap!"
Crackheads heap
swag on blankets for display.

Cheap, cheap
hookers seep,
swaying in stained lingerie.

Weep, weep
yourself to sleep,
as thugs pound Daddy, who can't pay,
and roaming pit bulls maul a stray.

Sleep, sleep—
the costs are steep.
Sell blow, get rich, and move away
to hushed and far Far Rockaway.

Andrew Hudgins is the author of six books of poetry: *Ecstatic in the Poison* (2003), *Babylon in a Jar* (1998), *The Glass Hammer* (1995), *The Never-Ending* (1991), *After the Lost War* (1988), and *Saints and Stranger* (1985). *Saints and Strangers* was one of three finalists for the 1985 Pulitzer Prize in Poetry; *After the Lost War* received the Poets' Prize in 1989, and *The Never-Ending* was one of five finalists for the National Book Award in 1991. His poems and essays have appeared in many literary journals, including *The American Poetry Review, The Atlantic Monthly, The Georgia Review, The Gettysburg Review, The Hudson Review, The Kenyon Review, The Nation, The New England Review, The New Yorker, The Paris Review, Poetry, Slate, The Southern Review, The American Scholar, The Chicago Review, The Hudson Review, The Missouri Review,* and *The Washington Post Magazine*. He's also the author of a collection of literary essays, *The Glass Anvil*, which was published by the University of Michigan Press in 1997.

Hudgins was a Guggenheim Fellow in 2004, as well as a Wallace Stegner fellow at Stanford University (1983-84) and the Alfred C. Hodder fellow at Princeton University (1989-90). He has received fellowships from the National Endowment for the Arts (1986, 1992) and the Ingram Merrill Foundation (1987). In 1997, he received both the Frederick Bock Prize from *Poetry* and the Ohioiana Poetry Award for lifetime contribution to poetry in Ohio. He was awarded the Hanes Prize for poetry from The Fellowship of Southern Writers in 1995, and in 1988 he received the Witter Bynner Prize from the American Academy and Institute of Arts and Letters. He is currently Humanities Distinguished Professor in English at Ohio State University, where he has taught since 2001. Prior to coming to Ohio State, Hudgins taught at the University of Cincinnati, University of Alabama, and Johns Hopkins University. Hudgins received an A.B. in English and history from Huntingdon College in 1969, an M.A. in English from the University of Alabama in 1976, and a M.F.A. from the University of Iowa in 1983.

Barry Moser was born in Chattanooga, Tennessee in 1940. He was educated The Baylor School, Auburn University, the University of Tennessee at Chattanooga, and the University of Massachusetts at Amherst in 1970. He has illustrated and/or designed more than three hundred books during his career. His work is represented in numerous collections, museums, and libraries in the United States and abroad, including the National Gallery of Art, the Metropolitan Museum, the British Museum, the Victoria & Albert Museum, the Library of Congress, the National Library of Australia, the Vatican Library, and the Israel Museum, to name a few. He is an Associate of the National Academy of Design, elected in 1982 and made full Academician in 1994. He has been awarded the Doctor of Fine Arts degree by Westfield State College, Westfield, Massachusetts and Massachusetts College of Art, and the Doctor of Humanities degree by Anna Maria College, Paxton, Massachusetts. He was nominated for the Chrysler Design Award in 2001. He is currently Professor in Residence at Smith College where he also serves as Printer to the College. He lives in western Massachusetts.